DEAD DAD JOKES

DEAD DAD JOKES

poems by

OLLIE SCHMINKEY

◇

Published by Button Poetry / Exploding Pinecone Press
Minneapolis, MN 55403 | http://www.buttonpoetry.com

◇

for everyone in the dead dad club—
you got this, and i love you

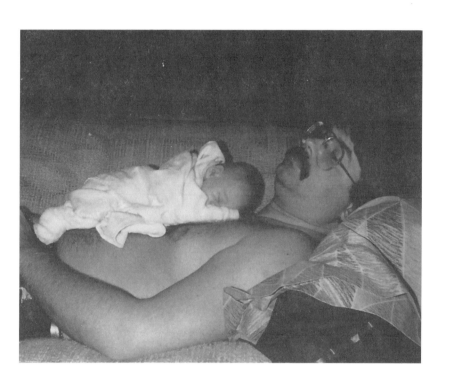

CONTENTS

DEAD DAD JOKES

I.

MY DAD DIED A WEEK AGO

and i search for a hawk. i test my gut.
i kiss the top of his urn like i kissed his dead forehead
in the moment after. the feeling of his skin under my lips,
chalked with cooling sweat.
i stand in the middle of a field and pretend to pray.
i chicken out halfway to belief.
i reach out my arms and pretend i
can feel energy pulsing in the wheat stalks.
i read my horoscope and go back to work.

my sister and i listen to the voicemails he left us
while we drive to the restaurant.
we listen to the voicemails
he left us.
i hear him in the crackle in the static.
his funeral flowers have barely begun to wilt.
that must be a sign?
there is a storm flashing low in the distance.
that must be a sign?
the wind on the back of my neck is warm,
and it must be a sign.

i touch the soft belly of a raspberry, and it feels just like his lower lip,
as i fed him his pills one by one just a few days before.
i pluck each berry, place them in my bucket,
and each becomes a new mouth,
a gallon's worth of him dying again and again—
i pick raspberries and smell the breeze and wait for a sign.
there is a spider.
just like there has been a spider every day.
nestled in between the brambles,
hanging from the side mirror of his old SUV,
dangling in front of my face on the car ride home—
i make believe my father is sending me spiders.
i make belief.

cremation doesn't actually produce ash.
instead, the skin and muscle burn away entirely,
leaving just the weakened skeleton,
which is thrown into a blender,
crushed, and returned to you.
my father becomes the margarita i want to order at the bar.

my father becomes snow.
after he died, the summer was gone,
and now, all i can do is wait.
i walk into his room and fold up his glasses.
they creak like they are still expecting a face.

his mother brings me a photograph
of him as a teenager,
and his mouth is open, wide with laughter,
and i am the one who doesn't exist.

THE QUARRY, SANDSTONE, MN

once, in high school, my friend Nate showed me the place
where he tagged the rocks in spray paint,
N and M 4eva, a graffiti promise
for someone he'd broken up with long ago.

last March, i took my friends to this same place,
and we climbed into a cave, which had an old gallon
of milk curdling in the stale spring ice of its throat.

i still come here even though i am grown
because there is something about silence
that only the woods understand.
there is nothing to do here but eat Cheez-Its and smell the pines,

and when i think about my father dying,
i see his body here, among the sandstone cliffs,
although we've never been here together.

this is a place i would come to kiss boys or hold hands
with girls or listen to the echo a guitar makes as it jitters
out over a canyon, but, still,
i imagine separating and burying each of my father's limbs
across the forest.

one, underneath the railroad tracks. one, on the bank of the river.
one, in the middle of the dusty parking lot.
and last, in the back of the cave, next to the old milk jug,
an arm probably, probably, probably, i would curl his dead
fingers around the handle
so that someone could find it, probably kids just looking to get high.

I WATCHED HIM DIE

i think the last thing he said to me was
don't pour water down my fucking throat,
but i don't remember because he stopped
being able to talk two days before he died.

this was a "peaceful" death, but, when they say
"peaceful," they mean compared to, like, being stabbed to death
with 600 tiny forks. the truth is, the body wants
to live, and so there is always gasping.

the truth is, he shit his adult diaper right before he died,
and so the room smelled like poop.

he had made me write it in his health directive
that i would cut off his hair and divide it into 3 parts:
1 for me, 1 for my sister, and 1 for my mom,
and we should hang it from our rearview mirrors.

i hold his ashes on my hip like he's a baby,
and the ashes are heavier than i expected.
i get him a beer and his favorite lawn chair.

my hands don't know how to sit still.
they want to be adjusting his glasses
and bringing a tissue to his nose
and pouring him a drink
and brushing his hair, and you know what?

i loved holding his hand.
i loved tucking him in.
i loved kissing his forehead before i said goodbye.

IF THE CELLS THAT MAKE UP HAIR ARE ALREADY DEAD

do they die again when the rest of the body does?

when the heart stops, how soon until everything else dies?
there must be a moment when the heart has stopped
but the blood is still moving, completing its final circuit.

and so when is the death?

if the hair is already dead,
and the blood is still moving,
but your father punched a hole in your door when you were eight,
who defines what forgiveness means?

the same year as the door, you watched your dog
die in the hallway. like your father's death, it was slow.
you watched the dying trickle into the body
at the same time the life leaked out.
the dog shit out everything, and your mother collected it
in old towels.

the body, in dying, cuts it all to essentials.
there is no energy to keep the shit warm inside the body,
and so it goes. the body tries to live every single second
before it can't.

in the car, it sneaks up on you. he's dead.
the knowing slides cold down your throat and into your stomach,
where it makes a burrow. earlier that day,
you spooned his ashes into an urn, and it felt like you were
scooping sugar into a cup of coffee.

at the bank, you smile while you hand the teller his death certificate.
you smile because you are supposed to smile
when you hand a worker anything.
you are closing his account.

his account, a door you have to shut,
maybe to block a draft, maybe to keep the mice out.

his heart stops, but the blood sludges onward.
he is dead, but his dog still needs to be fed.
he is dead, and in his dresser drawer
you find a Penthouse magazine and some lube,
an empty tupperware that smells like weed,
the titles to the old Mustangs,
a picture you drew him when you were six.

ERASURE OF MY FATHER'S HEALTH CARE DIRECTIVE

TO MY FAMILY, DOCTORS, AND ALL THOSE CONCERNED WITH MY CARE:

                     make   *known*

I want to die

        in the event of

                    let me die.

If at any time I should have an incurable injury, disease, illness, or condition

                                   let me die.

            I direct I be permitted to die naturally

If I am unconscious and on life-support machines
                let me die.

If

                let me die.

If

                let me die.
                let me die.
                let me die.

HIS FOOT

i find a portal to the afterlife in my father's infected foot,
his skin rotted away, a diabetic foot ulcer,
2-inch white and pink crater that foams
at the edges like a rabid dog.

he opens so deep the tendons jut up through the pus,
and they feel like the strings of a bass guitar as i slather
ointment on with my bare hands—
a quarter inch of skin gone, and nothing to do

but laugh like everything inside us is still a secret
that we get to choose whether or not to tell.

DEER SEASON

i bought his same brand of winter coat.
it makes me look like i could skin a deer.

as a child, i would walk outside after a fresh hunt
and poke the tongue flopping out of the deer's mouth.

i would watch as my dad strung the deer up
to the side of the pole barn, the weight of its body

thumping against the metal door. it sounded so heavy.
like it weighed more in death than it did while it was alive.

i watched my father grip the knife and slice the body open.
i can still hear the rip as the hide tore open for the blade.

the hot steam of organs birthed into the crisp fall air.
the thud as they became meat on the ground.

after, i would walk up to the deer and hold its hoof.
while the ligaments were still loose, i would open

and close the two hard black crescents. open, close.
and now, i get it. now that he is dead.

the elastic strung around his dead hair like a rope.
dead weight, how i lifted his head and it was so heavy.

and i cut his hair, gripped the scissors as his ponytail ripped across
their cold metal, a few stray strands planting

themselves alone in the sheets next to his shoulders.
how they didn't make a sound as they fell.

how he didn't make a single sound.

MY FATHER HAS NEVER LIVED ANYWHERE
BUT THE WOODS

and here, in the woods, my father drowns his teeth
in whiskey and teaches me a new game of poker,
and we play for dimes on the scratched kitchen table,
and i watch his hands trip over the cards,
and i watch his breath trip over itself,
and i know that somewhere else,
my father's dog has pushed her body into the ground without him.
he never thought he would outlive her—

and elsewhere, my father melts his bones
into the soil still holding her collar,
and elsewhere, he mistakes a tulip for a fist,
and elsewhere, he swallows every nest of spiders
before it hatches, so he can feel like he still has life in him,
or, just to feel all of the legs across his tongue like
a good strong wind, and my father,
if he ever had a reason to live before,
let me be clear,
he does not have one now.

the dog is dead.

look at this man. his large hands.
the soft spots where his calluses
have melted into his skin
like withering mushrooms.

he asks me if i'm going deer hunting with him next weekend
even though i've moved to the city
and been a vegetarian for five years,
and he tells me he's got a heater in his deer stand,
as if he thinks i'm afraid of the cold.

and i tell him maybe, we'll see,
as if there is any other way to be with my father
except standing over the body of a dead thing,
fingers digging for an exit wound.

here, my father begins to pack up his things,
i mean, his pills, i mean, he brushes the couch for her fur
and tucks it inside of mason jars,
maybe to make quick light when he is hunting,
or to start all of his fires,

and elsewhere, he holds a cup of coffee with steady hands
and waits for the earth to thaw,
for a golden animal to come running.

WHEN I HEAR VOMIT

i run *towards* the sound.
the bile sliding out of his throat and towards somewhere
i will have to clean it up.
if death is a fish, i have no choice but to be the newspaper,
to soak its blood while my father guts it.
cradle the gentle curve of its body.
when my father reaches the stomach with the knife,
he often unearths a sac full of orange eggs, half-babies,
and this one death blooms outwards into a hundred deaths,
and the fish's gut stretches out across the backyard,
becomes an impossible tightrope—

my father's death is always waiting for the applause.
it has planned its party and wants all the attention.
it is slow because it knows we have to wait. it is messy
because it knows we will have to clean.

it slowly peels my father's skin back,
to the muscle; his stomach unfolds—it moves through him,
starting with his blue and cracked lips,
stretches outwards and around until he is a skinless man
and i burst into a handful of seeds,
my body a hundred dead bodies
that will never grow towards the sun.

A HAND BECOMES

a thing only to unwrap from another hand.
a peel to throw away.
a rake to sift through the ashes.

the internet tells me my period blood is good for magick.
i don't know much about magick,
but i do know a lot about blood.
i fill a small jar with blood.
i fill a small jar with my father's ashes.
i wear them around my neck and feel immortal.

the glass bottles click against each other while i walk,
and it sounds like the same click my father's tongue made
on his last few breaths—his tongue,
fat and then still like the frogs we dissected in the 7th grade.

i hold his hand until it is time to unwrap the life from his body,
to unwrap my father from a corpse.

i keep coming back to this moment of dying.
how it was not like what i had expected.
there was no last word, no wisdom,
no wind, nothing to blow open our grief,
no soundtrack except the cough
of the man dying in the room next door.

some people say their dead looked so peaceful
they could swear they were sleeping.
for my father, it was the other way around.
for months, every time he slept,
i could swear he was already dead.

i actually started taking pictures of him while he was sleeping.
maybe half a dozen in the month before he died.
i needed to be able to *show* someone—

when i told my sister, she screamed and told me that she had
also begun taking pictures of him passed out on the couch.
we don't know why.
two siblings wrapping our fingers around our phones
while the light shrunk itself around his face.
i wonder if there is a word for that.
the urge to document the dying.

i didn't know my last picture of him
was going to be my last picture of him.
if i had, i would have made it something less creepy,
maybe one where he was conscious?

before they slid him in the furnace,
did they bother to unwrap his bandages?

i watched my dad die.
i watched a man die.
i held the hand of a dead body.
i was alive next to a corpse.
i laughed because i knew i would never be able to explain it.
my dad doesn't have a grave except the one inside my lungs.
i visit the cemetery anyway.
i sit next to the oldest gravestone and open up a book to read.
i say out loud, *hello*, and am always surprised when no one answers.

MY FATHER IS DYING

my childhood cat is 18 and has lumps all over his neck,
probably cancer. my father grows
new moles each year, probably cancer.
the cat is 18 and has probably cancer and can still walk,
and my father is 53 and has probably cancer but can't.
neither of them go to the doctor.

my father is not an organ donor.
there is nothing inside him anyone could possibly want.

i imagine his illness as a cricket,
only legs and a juicy body. i imagine how his heart pinches
at his ribs and frantically saws its legs together
trying to create a song.
i wonder if the friction is enough to start a fire,
if we could roast a squirrel inside of my father's chest,
man so sick he has become an oven,
body so full of lumps his entire family can feast.

that's all grief is, really.
realizing that you are too sad to sit with the other sad kids.
i know this because, when i say it out loud,
no one corrects me. but still they stay and watch me eat,
eyes following the juice dripping down my chin.

THAT'S WHAT YOU SWALLOW WHEN YOU LET YOUR GRAVES OVERFLOW

how many times you have dropped his body
only for it to surface again in a cloud of dust.
how many times you have ashed him into his funeral.
how many times you have replayed it over and over again—
the twitch, the shudder—
in all the versions there is a shudder and a twitch.
whenever you imagine it, he is in a bed.
he clutches his chest, or, he has long since lost consciousness,
and so his mouth hangs open like a grave as he sucks in each breath,
and it rattles like there is a piece of metal in his throat.

his sodium is critical.
you think about what that means—
to die from lack of salt while your salt drips down your cheeks.
you and your sister take turns screaming in the car.
she screams first, and it is high and full of gravel.
you scream when you are sure she has finished,
and you are low and growling like an animal
protecting its hard-earned meal.
the meal, of course, being grief.

as you scream,
you imagine his body tumbling out of your mouth,
a hundred times his body—thin legs, belly so puffy it looks
like it's about to pop, his purple feet—
his hundred dying bodies fly out of your mouth
as you scream, turn to dust on the dashboard.
you are driving to him, to ask him if he wants to go to the hospital
or if he wants to die from the low sodium,
which, if left untreated for a week,
would swell his brain with fluid until he seizes himself into a coma.

you have dreamed of your father's death the same way
some people dream of their weddings—
a milestone to mark time. the bookends of an era.
the portal into a new life.

his death is the threshold, and you are standing on a faded
welcome mat, peering through the doorway
into someone else's house.
they are eating dinner, all hunched around a large round table,
and you can smell the asparagus as you press
your face to the window glass—
they all look so happy, and well adjusted,
and satisfied with their meal.

but you don't belong in that house.
you belong in this one, with its dog hair and hospital bed
and pills and puke and dying.
you belong here with the dying.
you belong screaming into the air
as your father's death dusts your lips.
your sister says, *i almost hope he chooses to die.*
and you know she doesn't just almost hope it
but that she actually *does* hope it,
because it's been 5 years and we are all so tired.
tired of calling the nurse, calling off work, crying into a pillow.
tired of digging the grave so many times
our backyards have become cemeteries.

the last time you saw him, you rubbed lotion on his cold, purple feet,
and you clipped his thick and yellowed toenails.
when you pressed down with the clippers, the nail was so thick
it exploded into a burst of dust,
which flew up everywhere and into your face,
and you laughed, because it was so disgusting, and unexpected,
and fast.

A JOKE

my father drives an RV down to Missouri
because Minnesota is too cold.
the joke is, Missouri is cold too,
so he just sits inside the RV for 16 days.
the joke is, the campground he's parked at doesn't have toilets,
and he's already poured anti-freeze into all the RV's pipes,
and the joke is, now the toilet doesn't work, and the joke is,
my father shits in a plastic Wal-Mart bag
and pees into an old Kool-Aid pitcher—

the joke is my father can't breathe,
so he won't be home for Christmas.

i can tell he's lonely because he calls my mother
to talk for twenty minutes.
we ask him all about the plastic bag and the pitcher,
and, after he hangs up, we realize we forgot to ask about showering,
so we conclude he doesn't, because he can't touch his toes
without falling over, and, if he falls over, he can't get up.

i bet he sleeps with his shoes on.

in the best-case scenario, my father, in his stained sweatpants,
does not fall into a mountain of shit-filled plastic bags and die there,
because doesn't it sound like a joke—
a dying man drives an RV to Missouri, and he falls,
and he can't get up?

I FIND A CHUNK OF BONE THE WIDTH OF MY INDEX FINGER

it's not actually ashes.
it's 1/100 of a femur.
it's my dad's left shin.
it's the ridge on his cheekbone that disappeared when he smiled.
it's the curve of his jawline that i can see in my own face.

if only i had some glue.
i could piece together his whole skeleton—i've taken anatomy—

sometimes, i wear his not-ashes and tell people
they are grains of sand from the white beaches of Florida.
i have been on vacation.

on Thursday, i got into a car accident, and my hands
already started calling him.

i hung up before he couldn't answer.

i googled what to do instead.
i smelled saltwater inside my car.

one year, my dad accidentally spilled a bag of bird seed
on the lawn, and, a month later, we had a garden of wildflowers.

one year, i picked open a great gray owl pellet
and found two mouse skulls inside.

one year, my father died in my hands,
and i got a jar of white dust.

II.

WE ARE ON A ROAD TRIP

my father is driving. he is talking about wanting to die,
and he says he wants them to take his body back in a coffin,
and i say,
>   *well fucking let me drive then because*
>   *i want my body to go back alive in this van—*

if you take away my father's illness, you take away him.
if you take away my father's beer can, you take away the time
he showed up drunk to my fifth-grade play.
if you take away my father's beer can,
he does not show up to the play.

i know, when we are both sober,
i have no fucking clue what to say to him,
but on the road trip, we drink cheap whiskey outside of a hot tub
until we like each other,
or at least, until we feel like maybe God can wait to get our bodies,
or at least, until i feel stupid and brave enough
to tell him i date women—

and here, i am expecting the slap,
or him pushing me out of the van somewhere in Alabama
to let the Christians get me, or at least a lecture,

but all he says is,   *really?*   *well, i don't give a fuck.*

then,   *so which one of you is the boy?*
and i say,
>   *no one, dad, that's kind of the point—*

and we don't need to say anything else about it.

IF YOU ARE GOING TO TURN INTO A PILE OF ASH

at least warn me first. i'm going to have to take work off.
my father asks me how far away we are from the house.
    dad, we are in the house.
he says, *are the keys on the hook?*
      yes, why?

he can't drive, or really even walk, but he is always going
somewhere.
he talks a lot about going *home.*

my father walks with the walker.
shuffles.
i follow 6 inches behind him with the wheelchair in case he falls.
he still has a long gash across his shoulders from the last time.
the wound grins at me, the smile taking up his whole back.

he pees on the floor and then steps in it.
i sit him down in the chair and change his socks and wipe the floor.

    i want to tell somebody about this.

    i want them to hold my face
    and tell me i should never have to do this.

i look at the socks, a yellow footprint bleeding through.
the socks become snow, and my father is taking a piss
behind the van after we get home from the bar,
because he always liked to pee outside.

he is strong, and he can stand on his own,
and he tells me to look away,
because he is still alive then,
and people who are still alive get to have privacy.

the thing that no one ever tells you about dying slowly
is how much you must know someone else's body.
how many fluids can leak from it.
        pink, yellow, white, brown.

i've read the caregiver's handbook hospice gave us.
there is a section on medicine, on sadness,
on anger, on asking for help.
there is no section titled
        How to React When You See Your Dying Father's Penis.

there is no paragraph telling you not to stare,
not to describe it as, *chode-y and surprisingly wrinkly*,
not to say that with the catheter in,
it looks like an old person sucking on a straw,
        so you do.
because if you have to see your dying father's dick,
you should at least get to laugh about it.

        right?

GAY LOVE IS THE ONLY THING SAVING ME

my partner and i are sitting on our couch watching *Lord of the Rings*.
she is explaining each detail of where the movies
fucked up from the books, and i am holding her
hand and trying to remember the difference
between Boromir and Aragorn—

a hundred miles away, my father trips in the kitchen
and smashes his head on the countertop.
i imagine his face, how it must have peeled back
in a thin layer upon impact like sliced deli ham—

the heart failure spills vomit all over the carpet,
a line of bile dyed pink by pills and blood.
the heart failure buys him a nebulizer and lisinopril
and bumetanide and morphine—
the heart failure cancels my work shifts.
i spend 3 days every week sorting his pills and cooking him breakfast
and rubbing lotion on his feet and changing his diapers
and he is dying and i am angry.

because i'm here and he wasn't.

my 4th grade play. my father, absent.
softball game. my father, absent.
i need help on my homework, and he is at the bar.
college move-in. my mother helps while he is at the bar.
my father is a blank photo album—
the thing i most remember about my childhood is
the smell of beer and him telling me to never kiss a girl
because that's for perverts—

years later, his apology is absent—

if he's going to continue to be absent then he should
at least have the decency to be dead about it.

but being angry at dying people is never fair.
they need you. you're the one that's still alive,
and you can't leave somebody
in a puddle of their own vomit.
sometimes i want to quit, but then he'd die.
how can i go home if he'll die?
how can i watch *Lord of the Rings* with my girlfriend if he'll die?
when i'm there, i can't sleep
because the sound of his puking keeps me up.
i lay on the floor of my parents' living room
because the couch feels too soft, too much like my father's stomach,
and i can't help but feel my palm pressed into it
while my ear on his chest searches for a heartbeat—

i don't want him to die,
but i don't want him to be my father either.
i don't want him to die,
but i just want to do some regular fucking thing
like painting my nails or watching movies or being alive.
i want to do some regular fucking thing like being angry at my dad,
because other people get to be angry at their shitty alcoholic dads,
and i'm still queer and he still hasn't apologized—

so he trips in the kitchen when i'm not there,
and i don't have to leave my couch to check on him.
instead, my partner pets my hair gently,
like there's nothing in this world
that can't be fixed by petting my hair gently.
we are queer, which means
we have always known how to keep loving
even while surrounded by death.

and for just this moment, i get to be here,
where the couch is just a couch,
and i lean my head against my partner's chest,
and i hear her heartbeat, so steady, and strong, and here.

A POEM IN WHICH THE WORD *NAP* IS REPLACED BY THE WORD *GRIEF*

—after Nico Wilkinson

2 p.m., we all crawl into bed, my father in his,
the nebulizer on his nightstand, the walker within reach.

my mother likes it when i am next to her during the grief,
so i lie down on the big, soft bed.
my parents have had separate rooms for at least 5 years.

often, i am woken up from my grief by the sound of puke
hitting the toilet bowl.
i always abandon the grief, get up, check on him,
wipe his chin if it needs wiping,
clean whatever needs to be cleaned.

if i can help it, i let my mother sleep.
she needs this grief more than i do
because she lives with him and all the death
that crawls on him like fleas.
yesterday, i grieved with my mother in her bed.
she explained to me exactly how she gets comfortable,
a small dog on her pillow above her head,
another curled into her stomach.
she always rubs her feet together when she is really and
truly comfortable, and i've found that i do too,
like we're starting a little fire to fall asleep next to.
like if we try hard enough, when we wake up from our grief,
everything will be warm and possible again.

AN INCOMPLETE RECEIPT OF THE SHIT DYING HAS MADE ME BUY

3 new cups
a new cell phone charger
a pack of plastic cups
1 new tire
1 patch for an old tire
a new coil for my engine
diabetic socks
a 12 pack of size XL men's underwear
heavy duty garbage bags
new sheets
6 pack of Kleenexes
new sheets
energy bars
new sheets
Depends
printer ink
latex gloves
disinfectant wipes
$147 in take out
$2000 of gas
once weekly therapy for a year and a half
12 handles of vodka
13 bottles of whiskey
prescription for morphine
prescription for haldol
prescription for thorazine
prescription for lisinopril
prescription for spironolactone
prescription for bumetanide
prescription for metolazone
16 bottles of aspirin
an urn

YET ANOTHER POEM ABOUT ROADKILL

for people, we use words like, *distended, wound care, hypertension.*
for roadkill, we use words like, *disgusting, dead, wrecked.*
when are we saying what we really mean?

my father's bones disappear beneath his thick skin,
muscle replaced with water. he retains so much water
it bleeds from his skin, like condensation dripping down a window.
his legs swell like a hotdog in the microwave about to burst.
he breathes in short gasps, whispers, *please god let me die.*
my father drinks a glass of milk on the couch,
then becomes so weak his hands shake the glass out of his fingers,
and it smashes on the ground.
his feet are purple, like they have decided
to die before the rest of his body.
i rub lotion on his purple feet, all over the sores
that bubble up his calves to his knees.
i wrap his legs in new bandages, like they will hold him together.

for people, we use words like, *hospice, terminal illness, declining.*
for roadkill, we use words like, *fucked up, flattened, gone.*

my father is so gone he fucks up all of his pills, and
the morphine flattens his memory until he can't
even remember my name—

he always taught me that, when the dog can't walk anymore,
you take it out back with a shotgun.
end its misery, he would say.

i wonder how many things he has loved,
only to look into their eyes,
his large hand cradling their soft and greying jawlines,
lean the gun against their sagging stomachs,
and pull the trigger.

i wonder how their limp bodies fell,
if he hugged them to his chest,
if he cried,
if he dug the hole before or after the animal turned into a body.

i sort his pills by the hour and wonder how he knew it was time?

the only difference between a dead dog and roadkill
is that the dog was loved.
but its body will bloat the same if left in the sun—
its body will rot the same—
either way, all i can do is drive past—
my father's body is on my way home.
his body is on the way to the store.
his body is on the way to everywhere i need to go—
and i drive past, and the maggots bite into his eyes,
i drive past, and the sores on his legs widen,
i drive past, and his purple legs burn red in the sun,
and he splits, and the illness breaks a thousand
glasses until we live in a house of shards—

sometimes, i want to drag his body out back,
my small hand cradling his soft and greying jawline,
hold his face in my hand like a white dandelion
about to burst into wishes,
                        lean the gun,

                        and pull.

I AM LYING AWAKE THINKING ABOUT THE SPIT IN HIS MOUTH AGAIN

how we could have missed the dying
if not for the small choking sound,
like the first flap of a wing before
a bird launches itself into the air.

i pulled the wings off of a fly when i was seven.
watched it crawl on my skin, an animal reborn.
i didn't know it was wrong until Rebecca's mother
widened her eyes and told me i needed to kill it.

i imagine my father smiling and covered in iridescent wings,
slick like an oil spill, fluttering like a hundred old clocks,
and a hand reaches down to pluck one off,
and suddenly i am holding his shoulders while his head slumps
against my chest, his spit leaking out the corner of his mouth.

THE SCAB TO PEEL BACK

the bruise i let yellow into white.
i say *dead* and the crowd hushes.
i say *my dead* and the room shrinks
through the eye of a needle.
it says *i'm sorry.*
i laugh.
i laugh.
ash between my fingers just for me alone.
my dead for me alone.
stupid grief.
making dads out of cd skips,
gazes held too long.
stupid grief. time's up.
you're the hunted. you are precious.
you are spooned out.
what a thin meat you make.
what a soft sob.
what an unholy delineation of time.
every day is not an anniversary.
don't smell the snow and already begin to forget his palms.
stupid, to miss the way the skin hangs off of his bicep.

there is no one to remind to you to winterize your car.
it is over.
you are not fun at parties.
you think too much about sex for this to still be grief.
you're fine.
grieving people don't think about fucking.
grieving people think about their dead.
your dead.
my dead.
i want to pour ashes into my mouth when i am alone.
i have never loved my friends more.
i pick my nose in the car and maybe the other drivers can see.
my cousin henry sends me a photo of my father, and i time travel.

i glitch on his smile.
how i held his body, and so i know, but i don't know.
there are so many things to sort through.
i want all the fur and feathers.
i want all the things i want.
i don't cry anymore.
it is what it is.

I WRITE MY DEAD NAME IN MY FATHER'S OBITUARY

but we are not here to have a funeral for my name.

we are here to have a funeral for my dad, who died in my hands.

whose tongue gutted the roof of his mouth on his last breath,
whose spit congealed in the corners of his lips
like snow after a sloppy plow.

i write my dead name in my father's obituary.
i don't even think about it.

my dead name doesn't feel like such a *dead* name
while i'm standing next to my dad's corpse.

i don't feel bad about writing my dead name
in my dead dad's obituary.
what does it matter which name my dad used to call me
when he can't call me anything anymore.

in this moment, i don't give a fuck about what my gender is or isn't.
what people think it is or isn't.

there are some things that are alive, and i am one of them.

and there are some things that are dead.

HE YELLS FOR ME, AND I GO TO HIM

nothing has changed.
i am six, picking up the storm's tantrum in the yard.
palms overflowing with sticks, or, now, pills.
i am eight, clipping my father's thick and yellowed toenails,
or, now, bandaging his sores.
he yells, and i come running.
he asks for a beer, and i fetch it.
he asks for a pop with a shot of whiskey, and i fetch it.
he asks to be tucked in, and loved, and i do it.

my father has debt. medical bills gone to collections.
17 years of staying out at the bar.
my father has never had a job,
which made the transition easy, from
absent father to dying father.

ten, and he cries until 2 on a school night over the threat of divorce.
twenty-four, 2 a.m. water, 3 a.m. pills, 4 a.m. foot wrap.
my father's body is a clock made out of women.
my father's body is a clock that makes me a woman.

my father is a dying man.
dying, meaning, helpless.
man, meaning, violent.
and what do you do with a helpless violence
except fetch it its glasses?

my father is a sick father.
sick, meaning, dying.
father, meaning, absence.
what else is there to do with a dying absence
except arrive?
except cut all your work hours and shovel dog shit
off the cement slab?

there is a sleeping violence, i mean, a dying man,
i mean, your father, lying in a bed made of your small hands,
and so you must go.

when the dog, in heat, does not come home,
you must wander the dirt road until you find her panting
underneath the neighbor's bulldog.
you tell your mother that you could sell the puppies to pay the debt.
and isn't that it?
how only a litter of small bodies
could pay off everything your father has done?

THE FIRST BIRTHDAY HE IS NOT ALIVE

we all order his favorite drink.

we forget the hole he punched in the door.
the hole he shot through the dog.
he was so good at making holes, except when it came time
to dig one for his body.

there could be bones mixed in with our flour,
and we would never even know.
we could be eating cookies, and he could be
dead inside our mouths.

it feels stupid to be sad when he was mean for so long.
he only got nice when he was dying, and
i don't know if that counts as becoming a better person.

sometimes, i imagine him watching over me,
and i hide.

SOMETIMES I WANT TO HURT PEOPLE
WHO HAVE HURT ME

i post in the group chat that my dad died 20 minutes ago
and i get a string of 7 heart emojis.

the space between them feels like
the space between my own fingers where
his hand used to fit in mine.

there are more emojis on a dog video
i posted in 2017.

last week, i replied 6 hearts to someone
who complimented my shirt.

i'm 24 and my dad is dead
and everyone is busy going to work
and paying their bills
and going to class
and typing out novels about their favorite ice cream

and i sit there, with my 7 hearts,
each point digging into my arm
as i cry on my couch alone.

HOW TO BE ALIVE WHEN YOUR FATHER IS DYING

become everything everyone needs you to be / this is not the time for selfishness / or growth / this is the time to stagnate / moss over / become something alive that others can live off of / fill your belly with tapeworms / crack open your jaw so they can slide down easy / if you do not feel guilty / you are doing it wrong / everyone says they want to help / but they still want you / to show up to work on time / to be professional about it / you go to therapy and have long talks in the car / let other people complain about shit / you don't compare it to the death / because that's selfish / really / to let your sadness be so large it stifles other people's sadness / nobody wants to be around somebody who won't let them have a bad day / advice: shut up about the dying already, okay? / it's not new / we get it / it's hard / go cook breakfast / people who are alive cook breakfast / people who are alive support other people / and listen / and don't smash their heads against walls / or scream into pillows / or want to / fuck / you are a dead end street / dead / end / your dad would die in a week if he stopped taking his meds / your sister wants him to know this is an option / but how could he stand next to a cliff for 5 years / and not think of all the ways to jump / fuck / the amount of things he has lived for / or / the amount of things he has been dying for / your graduation / your sister's wedding / you put oliver on the diploma / and he made a joke about it / but nobody calls you by that name / don't mention it / you don't get to have anything / like a name / people like people who give / correction: people like happy people who give happy things / people don't like sad people who give sad things / people don't like sad people who know they are sad / who defend their sadness / so why don't you just not be / sad / or needy / or helping someone die / why don't you just adjust / build him a hospital / scrub away the beer / let me be clear: no one owes you shit / not love / or understanding / or a day off

THE LIFE OF THE PARTY

each inhale must also leave the mouth.
funny, how, if left to our own devices, we would
create so much carbon dioxide we would die.
funny, how, all the things we take in to keep us alive
would kill us when we let them out.

at a party, someone says,
i would die for another piece of that cake.
cake, white sponge, yellow frosting,
at a party
lol i'm gonna have a heart attack.
i would die for that cake.
i would die.

i do not clip anyone's tongue.
i do not make a guest of my grief.
i am looking for spiders, but no one cares.
i do not say,
if you are dying, then you have probably lost
the motor function to swallow a piece of cake.
i still remember the feeling of my father's
corpse, his soft hands growing stiff.

ha ha. growing stiff.
like a dick, right?
i am still the life of the party.
the *life* of the party, because i am *alive*—

okay, but i'm funny, right?
and i go to therapy, so it's chill, right???

i sit on the white couch staring off into what looks like empty space,
but really i am looking my father up and down,
and i am stuck in this moment,

the feeling of when he had just died but the oxygen was still going,
whirring and puffing, until the nurse said,
i'm just gonna take this off . . . since we don't need it anymore.

what the fuck am i doing at a party where no one wants
to talk about my dead dad—*stupid*—
and i think about where that oxygen must have gone after he was dead.
into the nostril, then, stopped by a closed throat,
fighting against itself back up the way it came,

or was it more like a flooded basement?
seeping into places you didn't think it could seep in?
going nowhere, staining the carpet yellow?

yellow, the color of draining blood.
white, death in his fingers.
yellow, the color of birthday cake.
white, as his eyes rolled back,
swallowed by the rest of his head.

MY THERAPIST TELLS ME THAT MY DAD WAS LUCKY TO HAVE ME AS A *DAUGHTER*

and i want to tell her to fuck off,
but i'm not very good at asserting boundaries,
which is one of the reasons why i'm in therapy
in the first fucking place—

my therapist misgenders me to my face
three days after my dad died.

at his funeral, i have to smile at people
who don't even get my fucking name right.

at his funeral, i make small talk with the same teacher
who told me he didn't think gay people should get married.

at his funeral, i use the women's restroom.

i don't bind because it might upset my relatives.

i am the perfect daughter.

speaks-when-spoken-to daughter.
cries-when-supposed-to daughter.
made-of-plastic-bags daughter.
duct-tape daughter.
eyelashes-made-of-clipped-toenails daughter.
pennies-for-teeth daughter.
copper-laugh daughter.
chapped-lips daughter.
dead-dad daughter.
dad-so-lucky daughter.
lucky daughter.

what a lucky daughter.

MY FATHER NEVER COMPLAINED

except once, he looked at me and said, *this sucks*.

he died on the 30th of August.
just like that, February forgets our grief.

my father's birthday is exactly one week away
from the six-month anniversary of his death.

i imagine his death as a baby. at six months,
it could be pushing itself up to sit on its own.

for his birthday, we are going to his favorite bar
to play pull tabs. i hope this will make up for

all the times his neck was too weak to support his head,
when his arms buckled as he tried to sit up,

when i wasn't strong enough to hold him.

my dad, never going to turn fifty-five.
or, his death, on the verge of learning to crawl.

III.

DEAD DAD JOKES

i think the sequel to the dad joke is the dead dad joke.

what do you call it when you cremate your father's body?
—i can't talk about it—it's un*bury*able.

why did we wait 30 minutes just to get into the crematorium?
—well, my dad was just *dying* to get in.

why did my dad get cremated instead of buried?
—he always liked to think outside of the box!

my dad died while lying down
—turns out he couldn't *stand* it!

if your dead dad doesn't show up to his own funeral, can you say that he *ghosted* you?

last week, when i scooped ashes from the big urn into the little ones to take home, my sister inhaled too quickly and coughed on her dusted tongue, and she said:
eating dad's dead body is disgusting—
—here, you have to try it—

GAS STATION

my sister's husband says he saw my dad at the gas station yesterday.
part of me thinks this is stupid,
because my dad is dead, and dead people don't need gas.
but part of me believes him, because i see
flickers of my dad everywhere—
his beard hugging another man's face, his eyes staring from a TV ad—
my car smells like him,
like body odor and motor oil and damp leaves.

once, a few days before he died, he slipped his hands
underneath the edge of my shirt,
and i felt his palms, so smooth and cold, each of his fingertips
like a worn rock pulled from the river.
his hands rubbed against my stomach and hips as he tried to find
strength to grip, to stand, to sit upright.

i keep coming back
to the softness of his hands, how they somehow worked their way
under my sweater, and how i was embarrassed for him,
the tender stomach of his child i know he never meant to touch,
his head sprawling away from his neck,
all his words turned to ash on his tongue.

THE GIRLS AT MY HIGH SCHOOL USED TO CALL SWEAT-PANTS "GIVE-UP-ON-LIFE PANTS"

when my dad stopped wearing jeans,
we all knew that he was getting ready to die.

often, the sweatpants were light grey.
i would put them on my father,
pull a grey t-shirt over his head and say,
Dad, you are making grey HAPPEN in 2018.
Grey on grey, fashion all day!

i used to be embarrassed to go in public with my father.
he always smelled bad, like beer and sweat.
when he started dying, he smelled like pee and sweat,
but a day he could leave the house was a day to be proud of.

i think that the opposite of shame might be love.
i don't know when it happened,
but, at some point, i began to care more about my dad than what
strangers thought of me because strangers are always
going to be uncomfortable
when dead people are walking around.

everyone on my father's side of the family can see ghosts,
and they know things they shouldn't be able to know.
my cousin looks at me and tells me i've got something special
about me too,
but i don't feel like i know anything.
i don't feel my dad holding my hand or watching over me.

i see an old man using a walker on the sidewalk,
and my stomach aches for those 30 years my dad never got.

if i die at the same age as my dad, my life is almost half up.

i imagine him sitting at a party, his arm around my pregnant mother.
did he know then?
could he feel his years stumble their way out of his body?
could he feel his life folding in half?

IT'S SNOWING AGAIN

it is my 2nd day of the week I'm supposed to drive up
and take care of my dad, but the drive
is too long, and the snow is too thick,
and so my mom tells me to stay home.

i remember my dad teaching me to watch
the rise and flow of the river to see if it was safe for canoeing.
he would always go fishing right after a rain,
because it made the fish more likely to bite.

i remember standing outside on our deck,
the mosquitoes humming around my head,
watching the northern lights flicker green and purple
across the sky, a river of light pulsing above me.

a different year, standing on the deck during
a dry storm, the lightning fizzling in bright
circles of light, like someone was hole-punching the sky.

the weekend my dad died, there was another dry storm.
and there i was, on that same deck
and watching the lightning grow arms.

i always hated talking to him on the phone,
although, when he got sick, we would talk for hours.
about mailboxes and the new county maintenance on the road
and the sound grouse make drumming their wings for a mate.

once, i asked him where he grew up, and he was so excited
to tell me. i didn't realize that because he never talked about it
didn't mean he still might want to be asked.
now, he is dead, and all i can think of are questions.

THE BAND-AID IN THE POOL FILTER

one time, i found a used Band-Aid in the pool filter,
slapping up against the ribbing like a fish gill closing.
i knew i shouldn't want to touch it, but the truth is
i did want to touch it, and the truth is
i *did* touch it, pulled it right off the filter
and played a guessing game about its scab.

      . . .

sometimes, i feel like one of the people who get to
go on *Oprah*. i am just tragic enough
that she would wanna ask me a question
but not so tragic that she would let me finish my answer.

      . . .

the only one i can talk to is my sister. i tell her that i've been mean,
that i said to someone's face i didn't give a fuck
about their dead cousin,
because cousins are like the loose change
you find in the couch cushions, at least, compared to a dad,
and i'm angry, because people don't know how small
their own sadness is,
and, for some reason, i think that they should.

i can also talk to my friend Jen because she is almost 40.
i want everyone else to grow up.
i want them to ask me about it without turning it into an interview.
i want them to feel sad but not for me.
i want them to feel sad for me.

      . . .

last night, i drove home and then sat in my car until the snow
covered the windshield.
i was a small thing in a small world being covered in thick snow.

the night before, i had a dream where i found
two giant spiders attached at the mouth,
and even in the dream, i thought of my father.

. . .

yesterday, my cat kept playing with a thread of a spider web
dangling from the ceiling, and i can never tell if i'm sad
because my dad is dead or if i'm sad
because i'll never get the chance to have a good father.

EVERYONE TELLS ME THAT MY DAD WILL ALWAYS BE WATCHING OVER ME

and i'm like

—*shut up, i'm just trying to masturbate*—

the thing is, every time i see a dick,
i can't help but think of my dead dad's dick—
and standing over my half-conscious father,
trying to scrub the blood off around the new catheter,
and my gloved hands peeling back my father's ballsack,
which was stuck to his leg and had created this horrible smelling
rash, which i cleaned and then rubbed with Gold Bond powder,
except i spilled the powder, ok, so we had to scoop out
the two cups of extra powder from in between his balls—

and it's not that i'm not sad that my dad is dead.
i am.
but i'm also saying that the first thing i said
        after i watched my dad take his last breath,
        after i cut his ponytail off of his dead head,
        after i watched his hands begin to turn yellow
        as his blood coagulated,
        after i hugged my mom, who just finished shaking
        and crying and screaming,
        after we joked about how horrible it was that the hospice
        had double rooms,
        so the dude across the curtain had to listen to my dad die,
        and presumably the dude before my dad, since my dad
        was only in the hospice room for 20 minutes
        before he was like *fuck this* and peaced out,

after all of that, the first thing i said was
        —*i love you dad, but couldn't you have died
the day BEFORE i had to touch your dick?*—

IT IS THE NIGHT BEFORE THE NIGHT BEFORE

the day my dad is going to die.
but i don't know that. all i know is that it's my turn
for the night shift, and he can't move his body on his own,
and he has had so much morphine that he doesn't make sense.
at least, maybe it's the morphine.

in his bedroom, there are 2 beds:
one is an old hospital bed from the 1980s,
tacky wood paneling peeling off the armrests.
the other is my old twin bed. there's about
a foot and a half of space between them;
the rest of the room is full of walkers and bedpans
and canes and his wheelchair and a vomit bowl
and supplies for cleaning his catheter.

i am not sleeping. i am listening.

i hear his bed squeak, and i climb over the wheelchair
to get to him. i say, *dad, do you need something?*
he says he has to pee, and i tell him he can just go,
the catheter's in.

he keeps on trying to stand, and i keep on trying
not to let him fall. all of his limbs are loose like
a rope ladder, and i have to brace my legs against
the wall, and he is trying to lift his arms, but they keep falling.
he tries to stand so many times i lose count.

after 6 hours of this, i think i hear him sleeping, and my body is so
tired i am sleeping and then i am waking up to a thump,
and i am running, and pushing with all my strength
to keep his sliding body on the bed, to beat gravity,
i know if he falls on the floor when i am alone with him,
i can't get him up.

at hour 11, i call my mother.
i can't do it, i'm not strong enough.

and she comes home from work, and i cry in her arms,
and she feels like my mother and not just a person
who is watching the same man die.

later that day, we decide to sedate him.
force so many drugs into his body he will lose
consciousness, if you can call this consciousness.

i know it is because of me, because i couldn't make it
through that night, because i cried and called my mother.
truly, i never wanted medicine's greasy fingers
all over his body—
we had let him die the way he was supposed to for so long,
and then, now, i couldn't do it, and god, what a betrayal.
to see the needle go into his arm and his hands stop twitching—

to know, now, that he only had a day left, if i'd known,
if i'd known he only had a day left, maybe i could have
done it, maybe, maybe i could have made it—

today makes 10 months.
today, i'm driving to my mom's house to clean
out his room. it has just one bed.

I NEVER WANTED TO BELIEVE IN GHOSTS

his ghost never yells.
his ghost never drinks.
his ghost never lets go of my hand.
his ghost is always asking to be tucked in.
his ghost loves me more than the addiction.

i want to be haunted like this:

> i want a ghost to leave a flower on my doorstep.
> to shut off the lights exactly when it's time for bed.
> haunt me, the tv flickering on to Jeopardy when i'm lonely,
> rattle the cookie jar, put the kettle on—

why is it the only thing ghosts are allowed to be is angry?

i think, of course, the spiders are a good sign,
come to eat anything that could bite me in my sleep.

my father got more kindness in his life than he ever deserved,
and i think his dying saved him
from being remembered for the way he was.

i don't believe in resurrection, but i do believe
dying gave him a second chance,
to be timeless in something other than violence.
for his hand to grow soft and become
the hand of a man i loved and not just the fist
that punched a hole in my door.

i want to believe in ghosts because
i want him to get better—
not from the things that killed him, but from himself.

REESE'S PENIS BUTTER CUPS

once, during 3rd grade, at my Catholic after-school program,
i tried to say that my favorite candy
was Reese's Pieces Peanut Butter Cups,
but instead i said, *Reese's Penis Penis Penis—*

in the moments directly after my dad died, i said,
do you think i could have one of his teeth?

and everybody looked at me like i was an 8-yr-old
that had just said the word *penis* 3 times
during religious education class.

once, while performing onstage,
i accidentally said, *while my fartner pucks me gently,*
instead of *while my Partner Fucks me gently—*

sometimes i say *dead dead* or *dad dad* instead of *dead dad*,
and isn't it just like grief to make someone more dead or more alive
just through a slip of the tongue.

a random phone number calls me at the coffeeshop, and i answer
because i think it might be the car place telling me my car is fixed,
but, instead, it's some telemarketer asking for DeWayne,
and i say,
i'm sorry, but you won't be able to talk to him because he is dead—

i apologize because he's dead.
i apologize because the person on the phone
won't get what they want.
i say *i'm sorry*, politely, like *dead* is their problem.
like my dead dead is their problem.
i say sorry like—*your loss*, they say.
i'm sorry for your loss, they say.

and i want to say—*why are you sorry did you kill him hahahahahaha*
but instead i say, *yaaaaaaa thanks*,
and they ask if he has an executor of his estate, and i say *yaaaaaaa*,
and i give my mom's phone number and then pick up my car,
which is done by now, and go home.

and when i say *home*, i do mean home.
except sometimes i accidentally type *homo* instead,
like, *love you see you later at homo*,
but i think, in this case, they both mean the same thing.

queerness, the only place i've ever been able to sleep.
where Reese's Penis Butter Cups just sounds like
a totally acceptable kink,
where i say, *what if i kept one of my dad's teeth*,
and she says, *i think it might not have been fun for someone to pull
that out of his dead mouth*—
and isn't that what queerness is?
to think of someone else's suffering even while you are suffering,
to circumvent their pain even while you slog through yours—

when i spell *grief*, i can never remember if the *i* or *e* comes first,
so i spend each day autocorrecting my *greif*,
my *grief, greif, grief, greif*,
until i can finally figure out what the fuck it is i'm trying to say.

ONCE YOU'VE SEEN IT

you can't go back.
suddenly you are a piece of grass
growing out of a crack in the sidewalk.
every day is a snow globe of his hair.
some days, you don't think you would have
loved him so much if he hadn't needed you so much.

you ask your sister if you can wear his old cutoffs
even though they are too big, and she says,
yeah, that's basically what gay fashion is, right?
and she means clothes, but you also know
it is to be dressed in the death of people you love.

your heart is a thump in the middle of the night.
you look like shit because you stayed up looking
at photos and examining your cheekbones.
you don't think you need there to be something after death.
you just need some chips and to stop fucking crying
so you can sleep.

reading about death helps.
so does watching Jeopardy.
it shouldn't make sense, but it does.

his shirt smells dank and stale, but you don't wash it.
you bury your face in it, like you couldn't bury his body.

sometimes you want to punch someone's face in,
especially if it is someone you love.
you want to be so full of good things you can take them for granted.

you don't want him back.
you don't even want the grief gone.
you want something else to happen.
you are bored, and you want to punch people

or dye your hair or just run for a really long time,
and the heat makes your skin slippery,
and your tongue is a slab of jelly,
and you don't punch anyone. instead, you go to therapy.
and besides, you don't even know how to land a good punch,
and you just want to hear the grasshoppers saw their legs
into a racket, hopefully it keeps you up—

you are tired of feeling sad, except when you aren't.
mediocrity pisses you off, and everyone is a terrible driver.
what would he be to you if he were still alive?
what fucking good would that do?

IT'S GOING TO BE OKAY

i knew it when i started thinking of it as
getting my money's worth out of therapy.
when i could laugh again.
when his eyes were again eyes and not just
shadows on his face.
when my mom stirred his ashes so they wouldn't
solidify into a solid lump.
when the dust flew everywhere and she didn't
even wipe it off.

i knew i would be okay because i have always been,
i guess. even when rape was the gospel preaching
inside my body. even when i came out and was handed
a bible dipped in blood.

i imagine the universe looking out for me,
the stars blinking like thousands of tiny lanterns.
grief is a thing which grows from love, not fear.

i pay attention to my veins now.
i can feel them sitting inside my arms and stomach,
and i know about death,
but i also know about loving someone until the very end.
the magic of a last breath, which is the same as the magic
of the first, where everything is dazzling and treacherous—

i don't think we need to live forever in order to matter.
i think we die and we are gone and our bodies rot
or else are burned and crushed up
and we go back to the world, except different this time,
sugar in a jar, plastic night light,
whatever's inside of an acorn that makes it grow.

I FIND A DEAD MOUSE UNDERNEATH
THE KITCHEN TABLE

i tear a paper towel in half
and through this blanket,
my fingers press against a soft stomach,
impossibly soft, so soft,
i want to bring it to my lips.

this body, impossibly small,
so small, i want to tuck it inside of my pocket.
a pillow of a body, curled paws like grains of wild rice,
a mug of tea steaming inside my throat,
how blessed i am to be the finder,
how this small creature did not trust me with its dying,
but how he did.

what a gift it was to hold the body.
what a gift it was to be able to hold his hand.

Congrats on finishing my book! I appreciate you so much, dear reader. As part of my grieving process, I also wrote an EP called *Dead Dad Songs*. You can check it out here for a free download.

https://ollieschminkey.bandcamp.com/album/dead-dad-songs

Love you forever,
Ollie

ACKNOWLEDGEMENTS

There are so many people to thank! This book (not to mention my whole poetry career!) is owed to a vast community of people who looked at me and thought, "that weird kid could be good one day," so buckle in!

Let's start way back: Thank you to Beth and Mariska for encouraging my creativity in high school and listening to my endlessly emo songs and poems and not laughing at me (it must have been hard)!

Thank you to all of the Macalester CUPSI teammates and coaches over the years—I'm so lucky to have stumbled into this amazing community that wasn't afraid to tell me when something sucked: Neil, Dylan, Sam, Rachel, Anna, Yashin, Ben Caroline, Cass, Danez, Hieu, E.J., Abbie, Natalie, Spencer, Wyatt, Becky, Talia, John, Kava.

Allison! A million thanks to you and SlamMN! for holding so much space for me and mine, and for continuing to make good poet spaces at Strike and beyond. You are such a pillar of this community, and I wouldn't be who I am without you.

Lewis and Beard Poetry—for publishing my first chapbook and not letting me name it "Toothpaste Oranges"—you were right, that was a terrible title.

Sam—I know you are a fancy publisher now, but I will always remember sitting next to you on the plane and figuring out my problems. Thank you for teaching me what you know about poetry and life.

My NPS teammates, especially Ry—thank you for validating my grief and letting me be a part of the dead dad club while mine was still kind of alive.

My folks at Well-Placed Commas! I love you! You are my favorite way to spend Sundays, and I am endlessly proud/grateful/honored to write poems with you each week. This book was written next to you, eating Owen's pudding cake (surprisingly not a euphemism), and I can't tell you enough how important the space we make together is to me.

My mentees and slam babies—you all are so wonderful, and I am better through teaching you and learning from you.

Kate and the Fox Egg Gallery—thank you for always giving my work a stage and a home whenever I needed it. I think very often of the magic we created.

Paul and OUTspoken!—for giving me my first feature and a found family that couldn't be beat.

Claire and 20% Theatre Co.—for giving me trans community and proof I deserved to be alive; for knowing I was good enough before I did.

My therapist Shawn (not the Bad Therapist from the poem, don't worry)—thank you for listening to my shit and laughing at my jokes and making your own jokes and understanding why I really needed to talk about my dad's penis in my book.

My dang friends!!! Asher, Ira, Koal—thank you for showing up to my shit and loving me through it.

My early editors: Natalie, Tyler—I respect you both deeply, and your feedback has been so valuable to me. Thank you for being people I could trust with this doozy of a book.

Xaundra, for loving me and my messy life. I love the time we spend together, and I love you.

The whole team at Button, especially Tanesha Nicole—you are a dream to work with, a top notch email-er, and all-around stellar human. I'm so thrilled we got to work together on this project.

Jacob, my sweet Jacob! I couldn't have made it through this without you. I really mean it. Eating pad thai with you with a face full of grief, your hand in mine with my dad's ashes in my lap—Every person deserves a best friend like you, and I'm so lucky to have you in my life. Thank you for loving me for so long and so good.

My mom and sister Leah—thank you for doing this with me. I love you both so much, and the only reason I made it through was because of you.

Trans people, queer people, thank you for existing and living and teaching me everything about how to love good, how to be loud, how to survive. I love you forever.

My cat Pete—you are every light at the end of every tunnel, and you make my life so much better. Thank you for living with us and being perfect.

Natalie, always Natalie, for being so good. Our gay life together is my favorite thing, and you are everything. Thank you for always being there, hanging around my grieving redneck family (and their 17 dogs), and seeing me for who I actually am. I would say more, but you already know.

And thank you to my dad, for becoming someone worth missing. Thank you for letting me help you die. Thank you for teaching me how to change a tire. Thank you for the luck at winning pull tabs. Thank you for inviting my partner camping, teaching me how to play dice, and ignoring all the rules. For crying when you felt sad, and for crying when you were proud of me. Thank you for putting it in your directive that I needed to cut off your hair and hang it from my rearview mirror—even though it was weird to ask for the scissors right after you died, I love taking you on trips with me (you're much quieter now). Most of all, thank you for the spiders.

ABOUT THE AUTHOR

Ollie Schminkey is a non-binary transgender poet/musician/artist living in St. Paul, MN. They facilitate, direct, coach, and host many organizations, including a weekly writing workshop called Well-Placed Commas, which serves primarily queer and trans writers. They've performed poems in 18 states, and their work has been featured everywhere from THEM to Upworthy. When they're not writing and performing poetry, they spend their time making creepy+cute pottery under the name Sick Kitty Ceramics. They are the author of two chapbooks, *The Taste of Iron* (Beard Poetry), and *You Are Sad and That Sucks a Lot*. This is their first full-length collection. You can find them touring nationally, making music, or playing with their cat Pete, who is always trying to eat things he shouldn't.

You can check out more of their work at ollieschminkey.com.

OTHER BOOKS BY BUTTON POETRY

If you enjoyed this book, please consider checking out some
of our others, below. Readers like you allow us to
keep broadcasting and publishing. Thank you!

Neil Hilborn, *Our Numbered Days*
Hanif Abdurraqib, *The Crown Ain't Worth Much*
Sabrina Benaim, *Depression & Other Magic Tricks*
Rudy Francisco, *Helium*
Rachel Wiley, *Nothing Is Okay*
Neil Hilborn, *The Future*
Phil Kaye, *Date & Time*
Andrea Gibson, *Lord of the Butterflies*
Blythe Baird, *If My Body Could Speak*
Desireé Dallagiacomo, *SINK*
Dave Harris, *Patricide*
Michael Lee, *The Only Worlds We Know*
Raych Jackson, *Even the Saints Audition*
Brenna Twohy, *Swallowtail*
Porsha Olayiwola, *i shimmer sometimes, too*
Jared Singer, *Forgive Yourself These Tiny Acts of Self-Destruction*
Adam Falkner, *The Willies*
Kerrin McCadden, *Keep This To Yourself*
George Abraham, *Birthright*
Omar Holmon, *We Were All Someone Else Yesterday*
Rachel Wiley, *Fat Girl Finishing School*
Nava EtShalom, *Fortunately*
Bianca Phipps, *crown noble*
Rudy Francisco, *I'll Fly Away*
Natasha T. Miller, *Butcher*
Kevin Kantor, *Please Come Off-Book*

Available at buttonpoetry.com/shop and more!